ROMANS

 LIVE WITH CLARITY

STUDY GUIDE · EIGHT SESSIONS

JADA EDWARDS

HarperChristian Resources

T0308498

ZONDERVAN

Romans Beautiful Word Bible Study Guide
© 2021 by Jada Edwards

Requests for information should be addressed to:
HarperChristian Resources, *3900 Sparks Dr. SE, Grand Rapids, Michigan 49546*

ISBN 978-0-310-11765-0 (softcover)
ISBN 978-0-310-11766-7 (ebook)

Cover design: Michelle Lenger
Interior design: CrosslinCreative.net

Third Printing in November of 2022 / Printed in the United States of America
24 25 26 27 28 LBC 10 9 8 7 6

CONTENTS

WELCOME

Beautiful WORD™ BIBLE STUDIES

ROMANS

⟫ LIVE WITH CLARITY ⟪

SOMETIMES the Bible can seem overwhelming. Where do you go for words of comfort when you're feeling overwhelmed, lost, or frustrated in life? What book of the Bible do you turn to for wisdom about the situation you find yourself in?

The Beautiful Word Bible Study series makes the Bible come alive in such a way that you know where to turn no matter where you find yourself on your spiritual journey.

The author of Romans, Paul, persecuted Christians at every opportunity. Then, on the road to Damascus (Acts 9), he had a life-changing encounter with Jesus that transformed everything. The scales fell from his eyes, and for the first time, he saw things clearly. With new clarity, he went from persecuting Christians to becoming one and building the church everywhere he traveled.

Before Paul wrote Romans, around 49 AD, the emperor Claudius decided to expel all the Jews from Rome. This edict remained for five years until the emperor died and his ruling expired. Paul addresses a shift in Rome, in which the Christian Jews are trickling back into the empire. This created a cultural clash for Gentile Christian churches who had been nurturing their congregations without Jewish leadership or input for years. Paul addresses the conflicts erupting from this change.

Romans shows us the power of the gospel to bring clarity to everyday life. It shows us how to love, how to resolve conflict, when to speak, and when to remain quiet. Paul provides a comprehensive overview of God's plan for salvation and gives us something that's like his own Damascus experience.

By diving into this beautiful book, you'll discover the great gifts of the gospel—the forgiveness of sin, the removal of guilt, the promise of salvation, the wonder of grace, the strength of forgiveness, the power of the resurrection, and the guide for walking with greater clarity through life.

> Romans shows us the power of the gospel to bring clarity to everyday life. It shows us how to love, how to resolve conflict, when to speak, and when to remain quiet.

HOW TO USE THIS GUIDE

Group Size

The Beautiful Word *Romans* video curriculum is designed to be experienced in a group setting such as a Bible study, small group, or during a weekend retreat. After watching each video session, you and the members of your group will participate in a time of discussion and reflection on what you're learning. If you have a larger group (more than twelve people), consider breaking up into smaller groups during the discussion time.

Materials Needed

Each participant should have their own study guide, which includes video outline notes, group discussion questions, a personal study section, Beautiful Word coloring pages, and Scripture memory cards to deepen learning between sessions.

Timing

The timing notations—for example, 20 minutes—indicate the length of the video segments and the suggested times for each activity or discussion. Within your allotted time, you may not get to all the discussion questions. Remember that the *quantity* of questions addressed isn't as important as the *quality* of the discussion.

Facilitation

Each group should appoint a facilitator who is responsible for starting the video and keeping track of time during the activities and discussion. Facilitators may also read questions aloud, monitor discussions, prompt participants to respond, and ensure that everyone has the opportunity to participate.

Opening Group Activity

Depending on the amount of time you have to meet and the resources available, you'll want to begin the session with the group activity. You will find these activities on the group page that begins each session. The interactive icebreaker is designed to be a catalyst for group engagement and help participants move toward the ideas explored in the video teaching. The leader will want to read ahead to the following week's activity to see what will be needed and how participants may be able to contribute by bringing supplies or refreshments.

SESSION
1

THE MOST
POWERFUL
LENS

ROMANS

Opening Group Activity [10–15 MINUTES]

What you'll need:

▶ Sheet of blank paper for each person

▶ Pens, markers, and/or watercolors

1. Use the paper and drawing/writing tools to draw a line down the center of the page. Then create a picture on each side using words or images. On one side portray an area of life where you feel you have the most clarity and on the other an area where you feel you have the least clarity. Consider professionally, emotionally, relationally, spiritually, etc.

2. Share your images with each other as you discuss the following questions:

   ● Where in life do you feel like you have the most clarity? What helped in providing clarity to this area?

   ● Where in life do you feel like you have the least clarity? What has hindered finding clarity in this area?

   ● Reflecting on the two images, which is harder to trust God with? Why?

Session One Video [24:30 MINUTES]

NOTES: *As you watch, take notes on anything that stands out to you.*

➤ **Romans walks us through four big categories: the righteousness God required, the righteousness God provided, the righteousness God planned, and the righteousness God expects from us every day.**

➤ **Paul uses many arguments to address the tension that he knows is happening between Christian Jews and Christian Gentiles.**

❯ Throughout this letter, Paul points us back to the Old Testament, because it's going to be important for the Jews to see that their God is consistent.

❯ The gospel was planned and promised beforehand through the prophets and Holy Scriptures.

❯ Paul says that even with our wrestling and struggles, and though we haven't figured it all out, our faith *is* changing the world.

❯ We all need gospel clarity to stay encouraged, live well, love others, and serve God.

Group Discussion Questions [30–45 MINUTES]

1. Reflecting on your culture, country, and world, what has contributed to the confusion and lack of clarity in our world? When have you unintentionally contributed to the confusion and lack of clarity?

2. Read Romans 1:1. Where does Paul find his identity? What tempts you to find your identity in things other than Christ? Reflecting on today's culture and world, where does your personal or political identity battle with your Christian identity? What do you need to strip away to make Christ your number one identity?

3. Read Romans 1:2–6. What is the gospel according to Paul? What are the benefits of the gospel (v. 5)? On a scale of 1 to 10, with 10 being high, how bold are you in sharing the gospel? What makes you hesitant to share the gospel with others? Who is one person you can share the gospel with this week?

4. Jada teaches,

"The gospel is the perfect lens we need for everything. The danger is that sometimes we treat the gospel like I treat my glasses. We take it off when it's inconvenient; we put it on when it seems to serve our purpose."

What helps you see life through the lens of the gospel? When do you forget to look at situations and people through the lens of the gospel? What can you do to remind yourself?

5. Jada says,

> "When we first fell in the garden, God knew right then that there would be a time where man would be reconciled and redeemed completely. Our God is not moment to moment trying to figure out what to do. God is watching his plan unfold. That gives us a blessed assurance."

When do you have the most confidence in God's redeeming plan? Where are you struggling to trust in God's redeeming plan right now? What practices help you rest in the blessed assurance of God's redemptive plan for yourself and those you love?

6. Read Romans 1:8–12. How does Paul express his affection and encouragement? What does it mean to be mutually encouraged by others' faith? When have you been most encouraged by someone's faith recently? What was the result? On a scale of 1 to 10, how intentional are you at building relationships where you can mutually encourage each other in the faith? How can you increase your investment in these relationships in the upcoming weeks?

Close in Prayer

Consider the following prompts as you pray together for:

▸ Clarity in every area of your life

▸ Gospel opportunities to share about Jesus

▸ New friendships to encourage each other in faith

If you don't understand the grace you've been given, you'll be stingy in giving grace.

Preparation

To prepare for the next group session:

1. Read Romans 1:1–15.

2. Tackle the three days of the Session 1 Personal Study.

3. Memorize this week's passage using the Beautiful Word Scripture memory coloring page. As a bonus, look up the Scripture memory passage in different translations and take note of the variations.

4. If you've agreed to bring something for the next session's Opening Group Activity, get it ready.

"Through him we received grace and apostleship to call all the Gentiles to the obedience that comes from faith for his name's sake."

—Romans 1:5

1

PERSONAL
STUDY TIME

DIGGING INTO THE

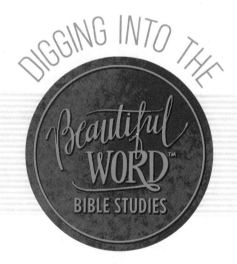

Beautiful
WORD™
BIBLE STUDIES

ROMANS
THE MOST POWERFUL LENS

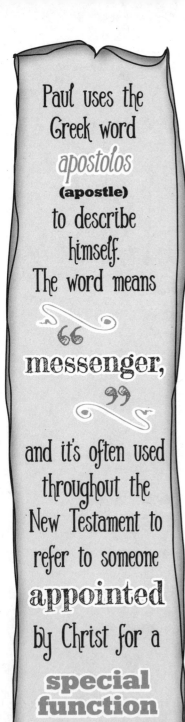

Paul uses the Greek word *apostolos* (apostle) to describe himself. The word means "messenger," and it's often used throughout the New Testament to refer to someone **appointed** by Christ for a **special function** in the church.

DAY 1
Romans 1:1

When Paul penned Romans, he had already spent the last decade spreading the news of Jesus through Greece, Macedonia, and Asia Minor. The fledgling churches he planted were growing, and he sensed God calling him toward Spain (Romans 15:23–24).

Like many of the New Testament letters, Romans opens by identifying the author. Before his encounter on the road to Damascus, Paul was known as Saul. The name "Saul" shifts when he encounters a Roman official in Acts 13.

1. Read Romans 1:1. The apostle could have chosen to use his Jewish name, Saul, or his Roman name, Paul, to introduce himself. Why did he choose Paul?

2. How does choosing a Roman name to reach a Roman audience reflect Paul's desire to effectively reach these people?

3. Read Acts 13:6–13. Up until this point in Acts, Paul uses his Jewish name, Saul. What happens in this story between Saul and the Roman official?

4. When have you adjusted your attitudes, actions, or attire to share the love of Jesus more effectively? Describe the circumstance. What was the result?

5. Reflecting on Romans 1:1, what are three characteristics Paul uses to identify himself?

-
-
-

6. If you were writing a letter as Paul did, what three characteristics would you use to describe yourself in relationship to God? Why would you choose these?

-
-
-

7. From the opening verse of Romans, Paul has clarity in both who he is and who he belongs to. In what area of your life do you most need clarity of who you are and who you belong to? Write a prayer in the space below asking God to give you that clarity.

DAY 2
Romans 1:2-7

From the opening of Romans, Paul declares the letter he is writing is all about the gospel of God (1:1) which is the proclamation of the good news of Jesus.

1. Read Romans 1:2–5. What names are used to describe and identify Jesus in this passage? How do each of these names and descriptions provide clarity as to Jesus' identity?

Paul wants the Romans—both Jew and Gentile—to know right off the bat that Jesus is the fulfillment of the Old Testament expectation for a savior. Throughout the remaining chapters, Paul will draw on oodles of Old Testament texts to illustrate this profound truth to Jewish readers.

2. How do the following passages point to Jesus as being part of the lineage of King David?

    - Isaiah 9:6–7:
    - Jeremiah 23:5:
    - Matthew 1:1:
    - Luke 1:32:

3. Read Isaiah 61:1 and Luke 4:18. How do these passages point to Jesus as the fulfillment of Old Testament promises and good news?

Throughout Romans, Paul uses several phrases or words with high frequency. One of those words is *called*.

4. Read Romans 1:5–7. What two things are you called to according to this passage?

   ·

   ·

God doesn't just call you to these, *he equips you* for them through Jesus. God is the one who calls, and God is the one who will provide everything you need to fulfill the calling.

5. On the continuum below, how often do you think of yourself as belonging to Christ? How does remembering you belong to Christ above all else give you clarity in life?

   1 2 3 4 5 6 7 8 9 10

   I don't think of myself   I think of myself
   as belonging to Christ   as belonging to Christ
   very often.   every day.

After introducing himself and identifying the recipients, Paul delivers a greeting that appears in thirteen of his letters: *grace and peace* (v. 7).

6. When you find yourself overwhelmed or uncertain, what role does grace play in helping you see clearly? What role does peace play in helping you see clearly?

7. Take a moment to pray Romans 1:7 over your life. Replace "all who are in Rome" with your name:

   To _____ who *is* loved by God and called to be his holy people: grace and peace to you from God our Father and from the Lord Jesus Christ.

Grace (charis)

is the

unmerited favor

of God
based in

relentless love,

and

peace (shalom)

is a

deep
wellness

and
completeness.

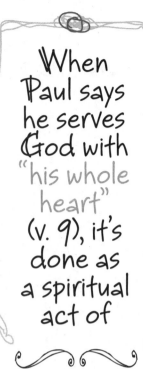

When Paul says he serves God with "his whole heart" (v. 9), it's done as a spiritual act of

worship.

_____
_____
_____
_____
_____
_____
_____
_____
_____
_____
_____

DAY 3
Romans 1:8-15

Paul continues his introduction and greeting by expressing gratitude and prayers for his recipients.

1. Write out Romans 1:8.

   What is of top importance to Paul in this passage?

2. What role does gratitude play in your relational life? How can practicing gratitude affect your relationships?

3. In the space below, make a list of four people you're thankful to God for right now.

   •

   •

   •

   •

Paul's thankfulness compels him toward prayer and intercession.

4. Read Romans 1:9–10. Reflecting on the four names you listed on the previous page, write a prayer for each person in the chart below. How does praying for others expand your capacity for compassion and care toward others?

PERSON'S NAME	LOVING PRAYER FOR THE PERSON

5. Reflecting on Romans 1:8–10, which of Paul's words are most endearing to you? Why?

6. Read Romans 1:11–15. What compels Paul to want to come to Rome? How will the visit benefit Paul? How will the visit benefit the Romans?

7. What do the following verses reveal about the importance of faith-filled friends?

Proverbs 13:20:

Proverbs 27:17:

Galatians 6:2:

Hebrews 10:24–25:

8. Describe a time when you've been encouraged in faith by someone else. In the space below, write down three tactics you can implement to nurture more of these relationships.

As you reflect on your personal study of Romans 1:1–15, what are the beautiful words the Holy Spirit has been highlighting to you through this time? Write or draw them in the space below.

SESSION

2

NO MESS
IS EVER
TOO BIG

ROMANS

Opening Group Activity [10-15 MINUTES]

What you'll need:

- ▶ Blank greeting card for each person
- ▶ Pens

1. Select a greeting card to reach out to someone who doesn't know Jesus and give the person a word of encouragement and reminder of God's great love.

2. Discuss the following questions:

   - On a scale of 1 to 10, how hard is it for you to share your faith with others? (1 = very difficult, 10 = fairly easy)
   - What makes it challenging to share your faith?
   - What avenue to sharing your faith makes it easiest for you? (examples: greeting cards, texts, emails, personal conversations, gifts)
   - Who are three people you can share your faith with this week?

Session Two Video [22:00 MINUTES]

NOTES: *As you watch, take notes on anything that stands out to you.*

▶▶ **#DontRushRomans**

▶▶ **Paul may have felt personal shame because of the way he had lived before because the gospel often makes people feel uncomfortable.**

> The English word *power* is *dunamis* in Greek, and from it we get the word *dynamite*. It's God's full ability manifested through the salvation and the rescue of humanity.

> God's wrath is a holy hatred of all that is unholy.

> In our culture, we love the human spirit more than we love the Holy Spirit. There's no amount of service, volunteering, or giving that will put you in right standing with God. It is only by faith and God's grace.

> In these chapters of Romans, Paul says, "We're a mess. And if we don't understand that we're fully a mess, we cannot fully surrender and fully accept the work that Jesus Christ has done for us."

Group Discussion Questions [30-45 MINUTES]

1. Jada says,

 "We have a billion-dollar capitalistic society that sells us products guaranteed to change us. But as human beings, we don't have the power to change ourselves."

   What's one silly product you've purchased that promised change but didn't deliver? Can you truly change your sinful nature on your own? When have you tried to change on your own and discovered that only through Christ is real change possible?

2. Read Romans 1:16–17. Describe a time when sharing the gospel has made you feel uncomfortable, ashamed, embarrassed, or silly. Describe a time when sharing the gospel made you feel grateful, empowered, and joyful. What made the difference?

3. Jada teaches,

 "God's wrath is a holy hatred of all that's unholy, and it's released against ungodliness and unrighteousness, not us. God already knows we are his beloved creation, but he hates unrighteousness, which is what we do by default when we don't have him. God's righteous anger is as holy as his righteous love. They are one and the same."

   How does Jada's teaching affect the way you read Romans 1:18–23? Without a healthy understanding of sin and God's righteousness, can you truly comprehend, appreciate, and respond to what Christ accomplished on the cross? Explain.

4. Read Romans 1:21. What happens if you ignore or reject God and his ways long enough? How do worship and thanksgiving help center your mind and heart on God? What roles do worship and thanksgiving play in your everyday life?

5. Read Romans 1:28–31. How have you seen one sin lead to another sin? How does sin cloud your perspective on life, relationships, and God? Give an example. How does righteousness bring clarity to your perspective on life, relationships, and God?

6. Jada says,

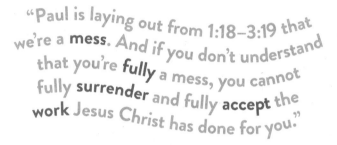

"Paul is laying out from 1:18–3:19 that we're a **mess**. And if you don't understand that you're **fully** a mess, you cannot fully **surrender** and fully **accept** the **work** Jesus Christ has done for you."

In what area of your life are you a mess right now? How can you surrender this area to Christ? How does acknowledging you're a mess make room for Christ to do something new? How does it increase your capacity for gratefulness for all Christ has done?

Close in Prayer

Consider the following prompts as you pray together for:

▸ Encounters with the amazing grace of God

▸ Renewed desire to share the gospel

▸ Clarity in perspective

God's righteous *anger* is as holy as his righteous **love**. They are one and the same.

Preparation

To prepare for the next group session:

1. Read Romans 1:16–3:20.

2. Tackle the three days of the Session 2 Personal Study.

3. Memorize this week's passage using the Beautiful Word Scripture memory coloring page. As a bonus, look up the Scripture memory passage in different translations and take note of the variations.

4. If you've agreed to bring something for the next session's Opening Group Activity, get it ready.

For I am not ashamed of the gospel, because it is the power of God that brings salvation to everyone who believes: first to the Jew, then to the Gentile.

—Romans 1:16

PERSONAL STUDY TIME

DIGGING INTO THE

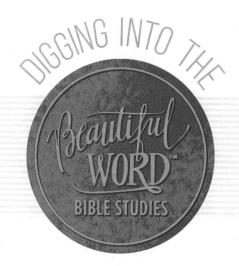

ROMANS

NO MESS IS EVER TOO BIG

In verse 17, Paul quotes Habakkuk 2:4, "But the **righteous person** will **live** by his **faithfulness**." The prophet Habakkuk **embodied** this truth **throughout** his short book in the Old Testament.

DAY 1
Romans 1:16-32

The first half of Romans serves as the introduction to the foundational statement for the rest of the letter. Romans 1:16–17 clearly states the theme of Romans and what Paul will unpack in the upcoming chapters.

1. Read Romans 1:16–17. In the space below, write the key ideas from Paul's statement in this passage.

2. Why is Paul unashamed to share the good news of Jesus? What in this passage empowers you to overcome fear and shame?

   What are three situations in which you find yourself ashamed or hesitant to share the good news of Jesus?

   •

   •

   •

After declaring the good news of Jesus and highlighting the fruitful, abundant life that comes with following Christ, Paul makes an abrupt turn to reveal what life apart from Christ is like. Those who choose to reject God and truth can descend into darkness and the self-sabotaging behavior that hurts themselves and others.

3. Read Romans 1:18–23. What actions is God angry with (v. 18)? What happens to the heart of someone who suppresses the truth (v. 21)?

4. How do worship and thanksgiving help realign your focus on God? What difference do you notice when you skip engaging in worship and thanksgiving?

5. Read Romans 1:24–32. In the box below, write down all the words in this passage that reveal the result of refusing to acknowledge, worship, and give thanks to God. Use larger size words to illustrate those that stand out to you or those you tend to wrestle with more.

6. The box on the previous page is full of characteristics of an immoral person who is rejecting God in every way. In the box below, write down all the opposites for each word you recorded above. What does a person pursuing Christ and loving God look like? Use larger size words to illustrate the characteristics you desire most right now.

Paul clarifies that the people he describes didn't make an accidental mistake. These are people who rebel deliberately. They choose to reject God and run the other way. This results in cloudy thinking and hurtful behavior. Yet the good news of Jesus is that at any point we can return to God because of what Christ did on the cross. We can choose to repent (turn around) and run into his arms.

7. What are three areas of your life in which you need to repent and ask God to forgive you and transform you from the inside out? What are three steps you can take to deepen your relationship with God this week?

AREAS IN WHICH I NEED TO REPENT	3 STEPS TO DEEPEN MY RELATIONSHIP WITH GOD THIS WEEK

DAY 2
Romans 2:1-29

In the second chapter, Paul shifts his writing style. Instead of speaking to the reader, he begins speaking to an imaginary opponent to make his point clear. This kind of communication, known as diatribe, was common in the Roman world.

He uses this style to illustrate that when we zero in on the faults of others, we can become blind to the faults within ourselves.

1. **Read Romans 2:1–4. Why is passing judgment on others such an affront to God?**

While judging others is forbidden, both Jesus and Paul call us to be discerning when it comes to our actions, others' teachings, and all-around hurtful behavior (John 7:6; Romans 12:2; 1 John 4:1). Discernment means to weigh the moral implications and likely results, whereas judgment often results in feelings of superiority or looking down on someone.

2. **Circle words below that are signs of passing judgment on others. Place a star by the words that are signs of godly discernment. Reflecting on the words below, how would you like God to treat you when you're in the wrong?**

Pride	Gentleness	Boasting
Humility	Condescencion	Love
Narcissism	Kindness	Smugness
Presumption	Scorn	Compassion

ROMANS 2:1–29 ADDRESSES **JEWISH PEOPLE IN ROME** WHO OFTEN LOOKED DOWN ON **NON–JEWISH** OR **GENTILE PEOPLE** FOR NOT FOLLOWING **THE LETTER** OF THE **LAW.**

3. Who is someone you're judging right now? How can you begin entrusting the person and the outcome of the person's life to God?

4. Read Romans 2:5–11. Do you read this passage as a threat or a promise? Why? What are the promises in this passage for those who seek the goodness and glory of God? How do the promises encourage you to keep pursuing God?

5. Read Romans 2:12–16. Jesus taught that it's important to be a doer and not just a hearer of God's Word. According to the following passages, why is it important to be a doer of God's teaching and not just a listener?

TEACHING OF JESUS	THOSE WHO OBEY THE LAW ARE RIGHTEOUS
Matthew 7:24–27	
Luke 11:28	
John 13:17	

For the Jewish people, the law was crucial to their faith and an expression of their love to God. For some, however, the obsession with the law to save became a form of idolatry, an opportunity to look down on the Gentiles and other less law-following people, and as a justification to skirt practicing everyday compassion toward others. Paul explains that any advantage of having the law and circumcision is negated by arrogance and fruitlessness.

6. Read Romans 2:17–29. Where are you tempted to believe that following certain religious rules, formulas, or schedules will save you?

7. What does Paul say makes a Jew a true Jew (v. 29)? Based on this passage, what makes a Christian a true Christian? Where do you most need to be transformed by the Spirit from the inside out? Write your response as a prayer in the space below:

DAY 3
Romans 3:1-20

After the initial opening of Romans, Paul provides a sobering indictment of humanity's sin. God doesn't show favoritism to Jews or non-Jews. He judges both by what they do. This argument would have stepped on more than a few Jewish toes!

A Jewish person may have asked, "Wait, then, is there any advantage to being Jewish?" That's when Paul says, "Why yes! Yes, there is!"

1. Read Romans 3:1–2. What is the advantage to being a Jew?

2. What do the following passages reveal about the advantage of knowing, following, and delighting in the law?

SCRIPTURE	ADVANTAGES OF HAVING AND FOLLOWING THE LAW
Deuteronomy 4:5–6	
Psalm 1:1–3	
Psalm 19:7–10	

Even when humanity fails to meet the standards of God's law, God remains faithful.

Some argue that acting in sin would just show off God's goodness even more. Paul quickly refutes this idea.

God's righteousness is based on his character, including his love, faithfulness, and holiness. The Old Testament reveals God's promise to save the world through the Jewish people.

3. Read Romans 3:3–8. What are some of the arguments you've heard people use to justify sinful, self-sabotaging behavior?

4. What are some of the arguments you've used to justify your sinful, self-sabotaging behavior? Which of these arguments are you using right now? What steps do you need to take to repent and change your direction?

Paul concludes his argument of the sinfulness of all humanity by drawing on a wide swath of Scripture. In the process, he reveals that his assertions are based on deep biblical truths.

5. Read Romans 3:9–18. In the chart below, look up the passages Paul pulls from as he pens his passionate indictment against sin.

SCRIPTURE	WHAT PARALLELS DO YOU SEE BETWEEN THE PASSAGES?
Romans 3:10–12 and Psalms 14:1–3; 53:1–3	
Romans 3:13 and Psalms 5:9; 140:3	
Romans 3:14 and Psalm 10:7	
Romans 3:15–17 and Isaiah 59:7–8	
Romans 3:18 and Psalm 36:1	

In Romans 3:10-18, Paul quotes from Psalms, Ecclesiastes, and Isaiah. He does not draw from the

Pentateuch—

the first five books of the Old Testament, commonly known as the

books of Moses.

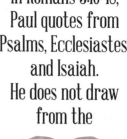

_____
_____
_____
_____
_____
_____
_____
_____
_____
_____

6. Read Romans 3:19–20. If the law cannot make us righteous or save us, what does Paul reveal as the purpose of the law? How does a heightened awareness of sin make us aware of our need for a savior?

7. Prayerfully read the Ten Commandments in Exodus 20:3–17. Ask God to reveal any areas in which you need to repent. Ask Jesus to forgive you for any sins and ask the Holy Spirit for empowerment to truly change and walk in greater freedom and holiness. As you do this, notice how the law makes you see sin clearly.

As you reflect on your personal study
of Romans 1:16–3:20, what are the beautiful words
the Holy Spirit has been highlighting to you
through this time? Write or draw them
in the space below.

SESSION

3

GOD
INVITES
EVERYONE

——————

ROMANS

Opening Group Activity [10-15 MINUTES]

What you'll need:

- ▶ Sticky notes

- ▶ Pens

- ▶ A nearby wall, window, or flat surface

1. Give participants three to five sticky notes each to write words of thanks for what Christ has done for them.

2. Place their sticky note prayers on a nearby wall, window, or flat surface in such a way that together all the sticky notes form the shape of a cross.

3. Discuss the following questions:

   - What are you most thankful to Christ for right now?

   - What about God's plan of salvation and redemption makes you the most grateful?

   - How often do you give thanks to God for his good and redeeming plan for humanity?

Session Three Video [21:30 MINUTES]

NOTES: *As you watch, take notes on anything that stands out to you.*

》 *Justification* is when God sees us as right with him because of what Jesus did.

》 *Redemption* is the transformation we experience as once we were slaves to sin but are now slaves to righteousness under the power of Christ.

❯ *Propitiation* is a fancy way of saying how we solve the offense of our sin against a holy God. Christ was the propitiation or appeasement of our sin for God, so we're justified and declared righteous.

❯ *Grace* is God's inexhaustible capacity to bless, to bestow on us what we could not earn and do not deserve.

❯ You can waver in a moment but still be considered faithful over a lifetime.

❯ Through Christ, we have peace with God and can rejoice in the hope of the glory of God.

Group Discussion Questions [30-45 MINUTES]

1. Read Romans 3:21–24. What is the good news Paul shares in this passage? Reflecting on the tensions between Jews and Gentiles from Session 1, why does Paul emphasize there's no distinction? Which of the following tempts you to make a distinction or look down on other believers?

   - Differing perspectives on worship or teaching

   - Differing denominations, types, or style of church

   - Different political beliefs

   - Different attitudes toward science

   Where do you most need to change your attitude and response toward others?

2. Jada teaches,

   "When Paul writes in verse 23 that we all **fall short**, he uses a **continuous** present tense. That means we **continue to fall** short of God's brilliance, God's standard, and God's glory. By nature, we are **opposed** to him and **never** meet the standard. The beauty in verses 24 and 25 is that we are **justified** by his **grace** through the **gift** of grace through Jesus."

   Do you to tend to focus your thoughts on the way you have fallen short in your spiritual life or on the way Christ has made it possible for you to measure up? Explain. How does your focus affect the way you live?

3. Where are you striving or trying to earn your faith? Where do you tend to compare yourself to others in your faith? What aspect of justification, redemption, propitiation, and the work of Christ is hardest for you to receive as a gift? Why? (See video notes for definitions.)

4. Jada teaches,

 "In Romans 4, Paul brings up Abraham, an important figure for the Jews. Many believed he earned his righteousness by perfectly following the law, complying with the moral code and by works. Paul refutes that argument."

Reflecting on Romans 4:1–4, what was Abraham heralded for? Which comes easier to you—following the rules or walking in faith? What gives you righteousness—how you behave or who you belong to? Why is this distinction important in Paul's letter to the Romans and to us today? When it comes to introducing someone to Jesus, do you talk about righteousness or godliness in terms of how the person should behave or who they belong to? Which is more important to you—how you behave or to whom you belong?

5. What spiritual practices or activities help you grow in your faith the most? What is standing in the way of you strengthening your faith more intentionally now?

Close in Prayer

Consider the following prompts as you pray together for:

▸ Overwhelming gratitude for all God has done

▸ Endurance in following Christ

▸ Opportunities to lavish love on others

There's no distinction for all who believe.

Preparation

To prepare for the next group session:

1. Read Romans 3:21–5:21.

2. Tackle the three days of the Session 3 Personal Study.

3. Memorize this week's passage using the Beautiful Word Scripture memory coloring page. As a bonus, look up the Scripture memory passage in different translations and take note of the variations.

4. If you agreed to bring something for the next session's Opening Group Activity, make sure to have it ready.

This righteousness is given through faith in Jesus Christ to all who believe. There is no difference between Jew and Gentile, for all have sinned and fall short of the glory of God.

—Romans 3:22–23

PERSONAL
STUDY TIME

DIGGING INTO THE

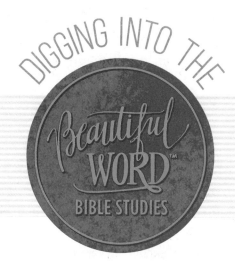

Beautiful
WORD™
BIBLE STUDIES

ROMANS

GOD INVITES EVERYONE

Righteousness

can be understood as a **right** relationship with God.

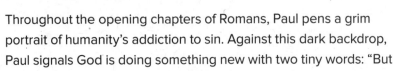

DAY 1
Romans 3:21–31

Throughout the opening chapters of Romans, Paul pens a grim portrait of humanity's addiction to sin. Against this dark backdrop, Paul signals God is doing something new with two tiny words: "But now" (3:21).

1. Read Romans 3:21. What is the new thing God is doing? How is this new thing still connected to the law and prophets?

2. Read Romans 3:22–24. What did Jesus' death and resurrection accomplish? Why was it necessary?

Paul goes on to explain that the death of Jesus was a "sacrifice of atonement" (3:25). Atonement is a reparation for an offense. Atonement sacrifices were made to cleanse the people from their sins.

3. Read Leviticus 16:6–17. What stands out to you about this scene of atonement? How does this parallel what Christ did on the cross?

_____
_____
_____
_____
_____
_____
_____
_____
_____
_____
_____

Instead of continuing with the sacrifices of atonement, Jesus *became* the atonement—a living sacrifice for the forgiveness of sins.

4. Read Romans 3:25–26. On the first continuum below, mark how much God desires righteousness or a right relationship with you. On the second continuum below, mark how much you desire righteousness or a right relationship with God. Who is more concerned about your righteousness—God or you?

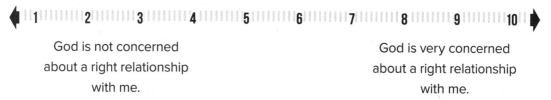

God is not concerned about a right relationship with me.   God is very concerned about a right relationship with me.

I don't think about righteousness or having a right relationship with God.   I desire to live every day in righteousness and have a right relationship with God.

5. Ask God to reveal where you're not living righteously or in a right relationship with him. Write a prayer of repentance, desiring a return to that right relationship.

6. Read Romans 3:27–31. How does living in a right relationship with God place Jews and non-Jews on equal ground before him?

7. Describe a time when you've felt confident you were superior to another Christian or unbeliever because of your actions or attitudes. How does this passage challenge you to be humbler?

Now **faith** is **confidence** in what we **hope for** and **assurance** about what we do not **see.**

(Hebrews 11:1)

DAY 2
Romans 4

To explore the importance of faith, Paul draws on the story of Abraham, one of the great heroes of faith for the Jewish people. Other than Moses, no other person from the Old Testament is mentioned more often in the New Testament than Abraham. This father of nations banked his life on the belief that God would keep his promises.

1. Read Romans 4:1–3 and Genesis 15:4–6. Abraham may have followed all the religious rules, shown kindness and compassion to strangers, and loved God above all else. What made Abraham acceptable to God according to these passages? What did God celebrate about Abraham?

2. Read Romans 4:7–8 and Psalm 32:1–2. How have you experienced the blessing of these passages?

3. Read Romans 4:9–16. Fill in the chart on the next page, noting some of the highlights Paul says about faith. Is Abraham's faith in the outcome of events, or in God who controls all events? Explain. Where do you tend to place your faith?

SCRIPTURE	WHAT PAUL SAYS ABOUT FAITH
Romans 4:13	
Romans 4:16	

4. Read Romans 4:18–25 and Hebrews 11:8–12. What are the similarities and differences in the way Abraham's faith is commended in these two passages?

SCRIPTURE	SIMILARITIES	DIFFERENCES
Romans 4:18–25		
Hebrews 11:8–12		

5. What obstacles did Abraham overcome? What obstacles are you facing now? How can you shift your focus from the obstacles toward God, who promises to be with you every step of the way?

6. How does Abraham's story demonstrate righteousness by grace through faith?

7. What aspect of Abraham's story is most meaningful to you right now?

DAY 3
Romans 5

Some scholars view Romans 5 as the conclusion of the arguments presented in the previous chapters, while others see it as the launching place for the next section of Romans. No matter your perspective, Paul's tone becomes increasingly hopeful and inspiring as he transitions from discussing the law and its merit, to exploring the wonders of justification and what has been accomplished through Christ.

1. Read Romans 5:1–5. What does Paul say believers can boast about or rejoice in? Describe a time when you saw someone facing persecution or struggles who used it as an opportunity to demonstrate loyalty to Jesus. How did this impact your faith?

2. On the continuum below, mark how you tend to respond to hardship. Describe a time when you encountered hardship and experienced growth in perseverance, character, and hope. Describe a time when you encountered hardship and did not experienced growth in perseverance, character, or hope. What made the difference between the two experiences?

1 2 3 4 5 6 7 8 9 10

I see hardship as a form of judgment or punishment for something I've done.

I see hardship as an opportunity to demonstrate love and loyalty to Jesus.

The Greek root for

justification, dikaio,

appears at least eight times **in Romans 5.**

3. Read Romans 5:6–11. How is God's love demonstrated through Christ on the cross? What have you done to deserve this kind of love?

Paul compares the way of Adam and the way of Christ. For Jews, Adam and Eve represented the source of human misery—separation from God, everyday hardship, and death that began in the garden once they rebelled and ate the fruit. This contrasts with the new life Christ offers through his sacrifice and resurrection—relationship with God, comfort in the Holy Spirit, and eternal life.

4. Read Romans 5:12–21. In the chart below, contrast the details regarding the results from Adam's choices and life and the results from Christ's choices and life mentioned in the passage.

RESULTS OF ADAM'S CHOICES AND LIFE	RESULTS OF CHRIST'S CHOICES AND LIFE

5. In this passage, how many times do each of the following words appear? How do the gifts and grace of Christ compare to the trespass of Adam?

- Gift:

- Grace:

- Trespass:

6. When are you most tempted to doubt God's love and gift of grace? What in this passage equips you to stand firmly in God's love and grace?

As you reflect on your personal study of Romans 3:21–5:21, what are the beautiful words the Holy Spirit has been highlighting to you through this time? Write or draw them in the space below.

_____
_____
_____
_____
_____
_____
_____
_____
_____
_____
_____
_____
_____
_____
_____
_____
_____
_____
_____
_____
_____
_____

THE SOURCE OF YOUR
SECURITY

ROMANS

Opening Group Activity (10-15 MINUTES)

What you'll need:

▶ A music player (such as a smart phone) with a downloaded playlist so you are ready to play a song that speaks of the allegiance to God such as "Jesus," "All I Have Is Christ," or "Take My Life."

1. Listen or sing along to the selected song. Consider printing out or providing a link to the lyrics.

2. Read Romans 6:1–4.

3. Discuss the following questions:

   ● What does it mean to you to live a new life in Christ?

   ● How is your life different because of Jesus?

   ● How does Jesus bring clarity to your life?

Session Four Video (22:00 MINUTES)

NOTES: *As you watch, take notes on anything that stands out to you.*

》 **Grace is not the license to do as we please but the power to do as we should.**

》 **If you didn't work your way into God's favor, you can't work your way out of it.**

What made you reflect? What

surprised you?

What caught your attention? What

> The law is not bad, but the struggle with sin is real.

> Don't be discouraged if you're trying to love Jesus more and still struggling with old patterns, old behaviors, and old ways of thinking. It's okay if you are in a healthy and persistent pursuit of righteousness.

> There's nothing in your past, present, or future that can make you feel condemned, because Christ does not condemn you.

> Rest assured, once saved, you're always saved; but that doesn't mean that there's not a wrestling in the process of sanctification—that's normal.

ROMANS 6–7

Group Discussion Questions [30–45 MINUTES]

1. Jada describes her time on a trapeze and says,

> "The **safety net** actually gave me the **freedom** to try things on the trapeze, to **want to do** what the coaches were instructing us to do."

On a scale of 1 (little) to 10 (great), how safe and secure do you feel in Christ? In your salvation? In the power of God's grace? Does knowing that God will always uphold you in good standing give you: (a) the freedom to do the things he's asked you to do, or (b) a burden thinking that those things are going to jeopardize your security in Christ? Explain.

2. Read Romans 6:5–10. When or where are you most tempted to live in willful disobedience to God? What have you found helpful in breaking free from sinful tendencies in the past? How do the promises of being made alive in Christ encourage and empower you to live for God?

3. Jada teaches,

> "Some people get confused because they wonder how grace works. They argue that if you take down the speed limit sign, you'd have more speeders. Paul argues that you **might**, but that simply reveals you have the wrong **motivation**."

Reflecting on Romans 6:15–18, when have you seen someone misuse grace? When have you misused grace? How does misusing grace reveal our true intentions and attitude toward God?

4. Read Romans 7:15–20. Paul is almost tongue-tied when trying to explain the spiritual battle within him regarding his sinful nature. In the last three months, when have you done something that you know you shouldn't have done? When have you left something undone that you knew you should have done? Where do you most find the war Paul describes raging in you now?

5. Why is it important for spiritual health to be honest about our struggles with sin? What happens when we hide those struggles? Give an example from your own life.

6. Read Romans 7:21–22. What does Paul do to strengthen his inner being? Describe a time when this strategy worked for you. When you're wrestling with sin, what helps you most to choose righteousness?

Close in Prayer

Consider the following prompts as you pray together for:

▸ The courage to trust Christ alone for security and safety

▸ Strength to do what is righteous

▸ Moments to practice vulnerability

The **struggle** with sin is **real**, but we have **security** in

CHRIST.

Preparation

To prepare for the next group session

1. Read Romans 6–7.

2. Tackle the three days of the Session 4 Personal Study.

3. Memorize this week's passage using the Beautiful Word Scripture memory coloring page. As a bonus, look up the Scripture memory passage in different translations and take note of the variations.

4. If you've agreed to bring something for the next session's Opening Group Activity, get it ready.

Now if we died with Christ, we believe that we will also live with him.

—Romans 6:8

PERSONAL
STUDY TIME

DIGGING INTO THE

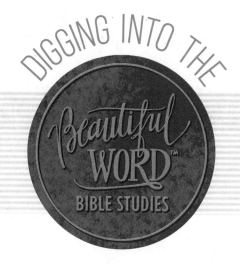

ROMANS
THE SOURCE OF YOUR SECURITY

DAY 1
Romans 6

Romans 5 concludes by declaring the grace found in Christ is bigger and better than sin. Now Paul expands the idea that grace doesn't give us reason to sin, rather grace empowers us to live into the fullness of life Christ intends.

1. **Read Romans 6:1–2. When have you done something sinful and reasoned that it was okay because you knew you'd be forgiven? How does Paul refute this kind of thinking?**

2. **Read Romans 6:3–4. In the box below, draw a picture or use words to describe your life before Christ and your life after Christ. Where have you experienced the newness of life (v. 4)?**

YOUR LIFE BEFORE CHRIST	YOUR LIFE AFTER CHRIST

3. Read Romans 6:8–11. What do the following passages reveal about what it means to be alive in Christ?

  - John 3:16–17:

  - John 10:10:

  - John 11:25–26:

  - Colossians 2:13–15:

4. Read Romans 6:12–14. What tactics does Paul encourage taking (practicing) to ensure sin is not your master?

5. Which of these have you tried? What was the result?

Paul says life is either lived in service/slavery to sin or to righteousness. There's no third way or middle ground. One form of slavery leads to decay and death. The other form of slavery leads to abundant life and holiness. One leads to bondage; the other leads to freedom.

6. Read Romans 6:15–23. Describe a time when you found yourself a slave of sin. How did you break free from it? Describe a time when you found yourself a slave of righteousness. What empowered you to live this way?

Is there sin you are slave to in your life right now? How are you a slave to righteousness right now?"

7. What is the result of being a slave of sin? What is the result of being a slave of righteousness? What have you experienced from moments you've been a slave of sin? What have you experienced from moments you've been a slave of righteousness? In the space below, write a prayer asking God to make you a slave of righteousness.

DAY 2
Romans 7:1-13

In the last chapter, Paul revealed how Christ's sacrifice on the cross frees us from being a slave to sin. Now Paul explains how Christ's death also releases us from the law. He's gone above and beyond to clarify that freedom from the law and grace should not be used to engage in harmful, sabotaging, or sinful behavior, but rather lead toward righteousness and holiness.

To help explain the binding nature of the law, Paul uses the story of a woman who is married, and then her husband dies. She is still bound by the law until he dies. It's important to note that this is not a teaching on marriage; rather it's a story told to illustrate Paul's point.

1. Read Romans 7:1–6. What changes for the married woman when her husband dies? What changes happen for us when we die to the law?

2. How is the new way of the Spirit better than the old way of the written code?

3. Read Romans 7:7–13. What is good about the law? What are the limitations of the law?

4. What is your attitude toward the law? How does your attitude compare to Paul's?

5. What makes sin deceiving (vv. 9–11)? How has sin deceived you in the past?

6. What is standing in the way of you living more fully in Christ?

7. What tactics can you take to remove every hindrance between you and Christ?

For the **law** was given through Moses; grace and truth came through Jesus Christ.

JOHN 1:17

In Romans 7:7–13,
Paul
uses the

past
tense

to describe his
relationship to
the law and sin.
Beginning in 7:14,
Paul shifts to the

present
tense

to show how his
relationship is
different.

DAY 3
Romans 6:14–7:25

The law exposed Paul's sinfulness and the tie to death. This prepares him to receive the gracious gift of Christ and his sacrifice through faith.

1. Read Romans 7:14–20. What is the struggle Paul faces? When in the last three months have you wrestled with a similar struggle?

2. Reread Romans 7:8–11. How does Paul treat coveting before encountering the law? How does he treat coveting as described in 7:14–20?

3. Why do you think the enticement of sin still exists after believing in Jesus? What situations cause you to be most enticed by sin? What can you do to lower your exposure to these enticing situations?

4. Read Romans 7:21–25. What does it look like for you to delight in God's law (v. 22)?

5. When have you recently felt the tension Paul describes in this passage? What did you do about it?

6. Read 1 Corinthians 10:13. What promises does God make to you in every situation where you're tempted to sin? How hard is it for you to find a way out in those moments? What would help you find that way out?

7. Who does Paul place his hope in regarding this struggle? When facing temptation, how do you respond? How can you follow Paul's example in everyday life?

As you reflect on your personal study
of Romans 6–7, what are the beautiful words
the Holy Spirit has been highlighting to you
through this time? Write or draw them
in the space below.

GOD'S GIFT
CHANGES EVERYTHING

ROMANS

Opening Group Activity [10-15 MINUTES]

What you'll need:

- Sheet of blank paper for each person

- Pens, markers, and/or watercolors

1. Imagine God's countenance when he looks at you. Use the paper and drawing/writing tools to draw an image of God's countenance when he looks at you.

2. Share your images with each other as you discuss the following questions:

   - When are you most tempted to think God is irritated, angry, or withdrawn from you?

   - Have you had an encounter with someone (a role model, friend, parent, etc.) that helped shape this belief? If so, describe.

   - When are you most likely to think God is pleased, delighted, and takes joy in you? Reflecting on Romans 8:1–4, what does this chapter of Romans teach about just how far God will go to demonstrate his love for you?

Session Five Video [22:00 MINUTES]

NOTES: *As you watch, take notes on anything that stands out to you.*

> **The Spirit gives us peace and power.**

> **The Spirit gives us presence, meaning the Holy Spirit dwells in us.**

> The Spirit empowers us to please God.

> The Spirit changes our position as we are adopted into the family of God.

> The Spirit testifies to our transformation.

> The Spirit helps us in our weakness.

> The Spirit intercedes for us, not intervenes for us.

ROMANS 8

Group Discussion Questions [30-45 MINUTES]

1. Read Romans 8:5–8. On a scale of 1 to 10, how much of your life is currently lived in the flesh? On a scale of 1 to 10, how much of your life is currently lived in the Spirit? Why are the flesh and the Spirit incompatible with each other? When are you more prone to live in the flesh? When are you more prone to live in the Spirit?

2. Read Romans 8:9–11. Why is it important to know that the Holy Spirit doesn't just descend on you but dwells in you? Describe a time when you experienced the presence of God's Spirit in a memorable way? How did that experience affect your love and gratitude toward God?

3. Jada teaches,

 "Living for God is an outflow of the Spirit's power and presence in our lives. When we walk in the Spirit, then we won't carry out the desires of the flesh."

What does it look like for you to walk in the Spirit? What have you found helps you to become more aware of the Spirit's work?

4. Read Romans 8:14–17. Jada shares that adoption in Roman culture meant the biological father first had to release the son (which has parallels to Adam and when we were enslaved to sin). Second, the family adopting had to pay debts of the child. Third, the adopted child had the same privileges as biological children. Finally, the adopted child was given the name of the new family. How does understanding adoption in Roman culture expand your understanding of what it means that you've been adopted as God's child? Which of these details is most meaningful to you now? Does anything prevent you from crying out, "Abba, Father" (v. 17)? If so, describe.

5. Read Romans 8:18, 28–30. When have you experienced suffering in life? In that season, did you tend to move toward God or withdraw from him? Explain. Did you tend to trust God was working for your good or question and doubt? Explain. How does the Spirit of God work in and through you in seasons of suffering?

_____

_____

_____

_____

_____

_____

6. Jada teaches,

"If God is for me, who can be against me? Nothing can come my way that brings defeat because God has already given me a victory. And he does it in 'all these things' (v. 37). What things? In the suffering, the highs and the lows of life, the questions, the doubts, the insecurity, the uncertainty . . . in all these things, not some. Why are we more than conquerors? Because we get the victory without fighting the fight that Jesus Christ did when he went to the cross and died, suffered on Calvary, and rose for us."

How does this change the lens through which you view suffering, pain, and loss? In what area of your life do you most need a victory? Spend time asking God to make you more than a conqueror in this area.

The Spirit EMPOWERS YOU to live for God.

Close in Prayer

Consider the following prompts as you pray together for:

▶ Heightened awareness of the Holy Spirit's power and presence

▶ Spiritual strength in suffering

▶ Victories in areas of struggle

Preparation

To prepare for the next group session:

1. Read Romans 8.

2. Tackle the three days of the Session 5 Personal Study.

3. Memorize this week's passage using the Beautiful Word Scripture memory coloring page. As a bonus, look up the Scripture memory passage in different translations and take note of the variations.

4. If you've agreed to bring something for the next session's Opening Group Activity, get it ready.

For those who are led by the Spirit of God are the children of God.

—Romans 8:14

PERSONAL STUDY TIME

DIGGING INTO THE

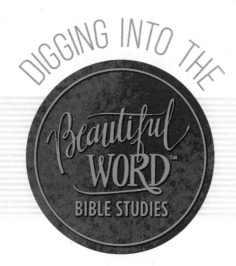

ROMANS

GOD'S GIFT CHANGES EVERYTHING

DAY 1
Romans 8:1-8

One of the mountaintops of Paul's writing is Romans 8, where he brings together his thoughts on justification, sanctification, and salvation to highlight the freedom and beautiful life that's found in Christ through the Holy Spirit.

1. Read Romans 8:1. Where do you wrestle with condemnation most?

2. Name a believer whom through your attitude, actions, or withdrawal you have condemned? How can you entrust this person to God?

3. Read Romans 8:2–4. In your own words, sum up what Christ has done for you based on this passage.

4. Which aspect is the most meaningful to you right now? Why?

THE mention of the word SPIRIT appears 19 times in ROMANS 8.

5. Read Romans 8:5–8. Paul uses the word *mind* five times in this passage. Why does the mind play such an important role in living in the flesh versus the Spirit?

6. What are some common thoughts you have that lead you to living in the flesh? What are some common thoughts you have that lead you to living in the Spirit?

7. Read 2 Corinthians 10:3–6. What does it look like for you to take every thought captive and make it obedient to Christ? In the space below, write a prayer asking the Holy Spirit to give you heightened attention to any thought that rises against God.

DAY 2
Romans 8:9-30

Though humanity has a sinful nature, the Spirit is the antidote to the flesh. In Romans 8:2, Paul uses "Spirit of life" or "Spirit who gives life" to describe the work of the Holy Spirit and highlight the contrast to the flesh, which is the work of sin and death. Now Paul identifies the Spirit as the "Spirit of God" and the "Spirit of Christ" (v. 9). We don't overcome the flesh and sin on our own; rather the Spirit of Christ lives in us. We are indwelled, empowered, renewed, and regenerated by the Spirit.

1. Read Romans 8:9–11. What does this passage reveal about the work of the Spirit?

Because you are his sons, God sent the Spirit of his Son into our hearts, the Spirit who calls out, "Abba, Father."

(Galatians 4:6)

2. What role does the Holy Spirit play in your everyday life? Where would you like the Holy Spirit to play a greater role?

3. Look up the following passages where Jesus speaks of the Holy Spirit. What does each passage reveal about the Holy Spirit and his role?

SCRIPTURE	WHAT JESUS REVEALS ABOUT THE HOLY SPIRIT
John 14:15–17	
John 14:26	
John 15:26	
John 16:7–15	
Acts 1:8	

4. Read Romans 8:12–17. Make a list of the rich promises of what the Spirit of God accomplishes in you. Which is the most meaningful to you right now?

Paul reflects on present suffering considering future glory. During hardship, he challenges us to enlarge our perspective on the great work of God's redemptive plan in creation. It wasn't just humans who were affected by the rebellion in the garden in Genesis; all of creation suffered, too.

5. Read Romans 8:18–25. What does it mean for you to groan or long for everything in the world to be made right again? If you could see one area of your life or this world redeemed immediately, what would it be?

6. Romans 8:26–30. What encouragement and comfort does Paul provide as you face struggles, sin, loss, and pain? Which is most meaningful to you right now? Why?

7. Reflecting on Romans 8:28, where are you most tempted to doubt this promise right now? When have you found this promise to be true in your past? How does remembering God's past faithfulness empower you to trust God for this promise now and in the future?

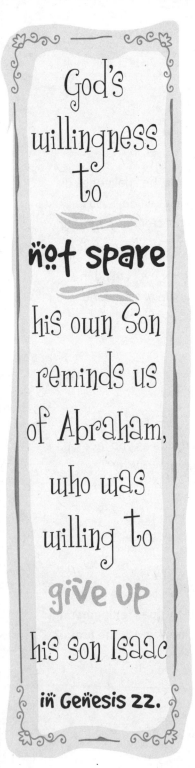

God's willingness to **ñöt spare** his own Son reminds us of Abraham, who was willing to give up his son Isaac ïñ Genesis 22.

DAY 3
Romans 8:31–39

If the opening chapters of Romans focused on the overwhelming hard news of humanity's sinful state, the closing of Romans 8 erupts in a joyful celebration of who we are in Christ and God's unfathomable love for us.

1. Read Romans 8:31. In the space below, write down three different situations, circumstances, or people who you feel are against you and may be bringing out the worst in you.

   •

   •

   •

When Paul says God is for you, that doesn't mean that you'll always win in earthly terms, but rather that God is for your whole redemption, renewal, and regeneration in Christ through the Spirit.

2. Reflecting on the three situations, circumstances, or people who you feel are against you, how could each one be used by God to help you grow in dependence on the Spirit and become more like Jesus?

   •

   •

   •

3. Read Romans 8:32–34. On the continuum below, mark how much you trust God will graciously give you what you need. In what areas are you most tempted to doubt God as your provider? What planted that seed of doubt?

◀ 1 | 2 | 3 | 4 | 5 | 6 | 7 | 8 | 9 | 10 ▶

I often doubt that God will give me what I need.

I always trust that God will give me what I need.

4. Read Romans 8:35. Rank the following 1–7 according to which one hurts you most. Then rank the following 1–7 on which tempts you to doubt God's love most. Describe any connections between the severity of your pain and the amount of doubt it spurs toward God.

HURTS THE MOST	SITUATIONS	DOUBT GOD THE MOST
	Sticky situations (trouble)	
	Loss, pain, and suffering (hardship}	
	Retaliation for faith (persecution}	
	Lack of provision (famine)	
	Vulnerability that leads to rejection (nakedness)	
	Physical/emotional trauma and threats (danger)	
	Sudden death of someone you love (love)	

5. Read Romans 8:36; Psalm 44:22; and John 16:33. Why is it tempting to think that being a follower of Jesus gives you an exemption to suffering? What do these passages reveal about suffering? What comfort do you find in knowing you are not alone in your suffering and that generations of followers of God, and even Jesus, have encountered suffering?

6. Read Romans 8:37–39. To be in Christ and filled with the Spirit means that you are forever anchored in God's love. On the continuum below, mark how much you feel secure in Christ's love today.

◀ 1 2 3 4 5 6 7 8 9 10 ▶

I don't feel secure in
Christ's love very often.

I feel super secure in
Christ's love every day.

7. How does knowing you're securely loved by Christ affect each of the following? How can you nurture a deeper sense of God's great love for you in these areas?

Your emotions:

Your outlook on life:

Your attitude:

Your relationships with others:

As you reflect on your personal study of Romans 8, what are the beautiful words the Holy Spirit has been highlighting to you through this time? Write or draw them in the space below.

_____

_____

_____

_____

_____

_____

_____

_____

_____

_____

_____

_____

_____

_____

_____

_____

_____

_____

_____

_____

_____

SESSION
6

GOD KEEPS
EVERY PROMISE

ROMANS

Opening Group Activity [10-15 MINUTES]

What you'll need:

- ▶ Sheet of blank paper for each person

- ▶ Pens

1. Create two columns on their paper. Mark the first column, "People I'd love to see experience and know Jesus." Mark the second column, "People I'd love to see return to Jesus."

2. Spend some time in prayer asking God to reveal himself to each person and draw them back to himself. Discuss the following questions:

   - When have you seen someone recently come to faith in Christ?

   - When have you seen someone return to Christ who had wandered from him?

   - How does sharing your faith with others strengthen your own faith?

Session Six Video [24:00 MINUTES]

NOTES: *As you watch, take notes on anything that stands out to you.*

» **Paul shares his burden and the history of God's plan of salvation for Israel.**

» **Because you are part of a particular ethnic group doesn't mean you have chosen to be governed by God.**

❯ To have days of health and joy and goodness around us is the overwhelming grace of God because those days are undeserved.

❯ Don't take God's grace, his goodness, and his sovereignty to mean you have no responsibility. We still are responsible for the lives that we choose to live.

❯ We are all preachers. We are all responsible for proclaiming this truth.

❯ Be grateful to be a part of God's plan! How magnificent that we, the Gentiles, the wild olive shoots, are being used by God to reinvigorate his people so they can ultimately choose him.

ROMAN 9–11

Group Discussion Questions [30-45 MINUTES]

1. Read Romans 9:1–5. Why is Paul so heartbroken over the Jewish people who don't recognize Jesus as the long-awaited Messiah? Who are those unbelievers that you feel most heartbroken about?

2. Jada teaches,

"Paul's fellow Jews were often his worst enemies. They oversaw a lot of his torture and persecution as he was trying to spread the gospel of Jesus Christ, but he still had a burden for them."

Like Paul, how do you have a gospel-centered grief even for those who hurt you? How can you have a burden for people who offend you and cause you pain? How can you nurture a greater desire that such people come to salvation?

3. Read Romans 9:14–18. How does Paul answer his own question regarding God's justice? What characteristics of God are described in this passage?

4. In what area have you allowed your heart to become hard? How do you want God to respond to you?

5. Jada teaches,

"When people ask, 'Why didn't God heal my mom or dad?' or 'Why didn't God prevent bad things from happening?' We must start from a point of compassion because those are legitimate questions. I try to bridge this gap by helping them understand from Romans 1 that we as humans are deserving of wrath by default. The fact that we have anything good at all is grace, because everything good is undeserved. When people ask, 'How can God allow suffering?' I ask, 'How can God give grace?' I approach from the other end: it's not why do bad things happen, but 'God, I can't believe you allow so many good things to happen!'"

How does Jada's teaching make you think about suffering and loss differently? How do you respond to people who ask, "Why do bad things happen to good people?" in light of Romans?

6. Read Romans 11:17–18. Jada teaches that if an olive tree was old and lost its vigor, one of the remedies was to take new olive shoots and graft them in. Over time, these would reinvigorate the entire olive branch and it would come back to life. How does God's grafting of the Gentile believers help bring back life to the Jewish people? What surprises you most about God's plan? Where do you see grafting today? Why do the Gentiles need to remain humble? Where are you most tempted by arrogance or pride in your spiritual journey?

7. Read Romans 11:33–37. What characteristics of God are mentioned in this passage? How does God's plan for the Jews and Gentiles demonstrate these characteristics? On a scale of 1 to 10, how comfortable are you with the idea that God is mysterious, that his ways are higher than our ways? What do you love about God's mysterious ways? What challenges you most about God's mysterious ways?

Close in Prayer

Consider the following prompts as you pray together for:

▶ Forgiveness toward those who have caused harm

▶ Humility to love others well

▶ Fresh opportunities to share the good news of Christ

The **great commission** is **universal;** it's for **every believer.**

Preparation

To prepare for the next group session:

1. Read Romans 9–11.

2. Tackle the three days of the Session 6 Personal Study.

3. Memorize this week's passage using the Beautiful Word Scripture memory coloring page. As a bonus, look up the Scripture memory passage in different translations and take note of the variations.

For he says to Moses, "I will have mercy on whom I have mercy, and will have compassion on whom I have compassion."

—Romans 9:15

PERSONAL STUDY TIME

DIGGING INTO THE

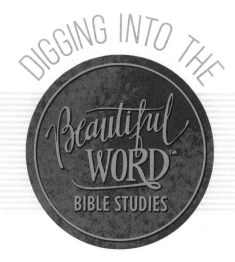

ROMANS
GOD KEEPS EVERY PROMISE

In the **great story** of God freeing the Israelites from the rule of **Pharoah,** the **hardening** of Pharoah's **heart** appears **twenty times** in Exodus 4-14.

DAY 1
Romans 9

Paul wants everyone to receive the breathtaking news of salvation through Jesus Christ. Yet he finds himself in a conundrum. Non-Jews are flocking to know Christ, but his own people are barely trickling in. This leaves Paul heartbroken as he aches for everyone to know Jesus and receive salvation.

In Romans 9, he wrestles with the question of what God is up to. If God called, chose, adopted, and promised the Jewish people that he would save them, and if the Messiah has come, then what went wrong? Did God break his promises? Did God's plan go awry?

1. Read Romans 9:1–5. What is the source of Paul's anguish?

2. Read Romans 9:6–13. What Old Testament stories, which would have been very familiar to a Jewish audience, does Paul refer to in this passage? How do these stories illustrate that God did not fail? How do these stories reveal that God is acting in the same ways toward Paul's fellow Jews?

It's worth noting that in the story of the two brothers, God does not wait for them to grow and mature into grown adults. God's selection is not based on achievement or character or worthiness. The decision was made by God while the boys were still in the womb. Therefore, God's election or selection is based on God's character, wisdom, and purposes. Long before God gave humanity free choice, God had free choice.

3. Read Romans 9:14–18. What characteristics of God are described in this passage? Which are the most meaningful to you now?

God's expression of mercy means that when it comes to justice, God will give someone what they don't deserve and withhold what they do deserve.

4. What comfort do you find in God's free choice? What challenges you in God having free choice in his actions?

God takes a long-term approach to his love and mercy. He loves to show compassion—both to Jews and non-Jews—and does it with remarkable patience.

5. Read Romans 8:19–29. How has God demonstrated his compassion, patience, and mercy to you?

The irony is that Gentiles who didn't believe in righteousness are being made right with God through faith, and that Jews who engaged the law as a means of righteousness have missed out because they thought their works could save them. After exploring God's freedom of choice, Paul returns to the core issues of righteousness and faith.

> "The fact that God has chosen some to be saved does not mean that he has chosen the rest to be lost. The world is already lost and dead in sins. If left to us, all of us would be condemned eternally. The question is, Does God have a right to stoop down, take a handful of already doomed clay, and fashion a vessel of beauty out of it? Of course, he does." [1]
>
> Max Lucado, pastor and author

6. Read Romans 8:30–33. In what area of your spiritual life are you doing something because secretly you're wanting to earn God's favor, affection, or salvation, or you feel as if you owe God something? How can you change your attitude and perspective to reflect Paul's teaching in this passage?

7. Where is your stumbling block in the gospel? What's the hardest part of believing that God, Jesus, and the Holy Spirit are for you? Why?

DAY 2
Romans 10

Once again Paul expresses heartfelt concern for his Jewish community.

1. Read Romans 10:1–2. How can religious zeal driven by ignorance do harm? When have you ever encountered someone who in wild zeal for God acted in unhealthy or harmful attitudes or manners? In your zeal for God, when have you ever done something that you look back and regret because it caused harm to yourself or others?

Paul says that his Jewish community has been working so hard to be right with God that they established their own way to do it—often through layers and layers of the law. In essence, they missed the forest through the trees. They worked so hard for righteous standing that they refused to submit and receive God's righteousness through Christ. Despite their special relationship with God and following the law, Jesus arrives, and they reject him.

2. Read Romans 10:3–4. Where are you prone to striving in your relationship with God? How does this passage challenge you to grow in your faith?

3. Read Romans 10:5–13. How do you experience salvation according to this passage?

4. It's easy to say we are saved through Christ, but sometimes our attitudes and actions reveal we think we need to add something to our spiritual lives to ensure salvation or favor with God. Reflect on the sentence and options below. Circle those which you're tempted to lean on or use as a just-in-case backup plan to receive God's salvation or favor.

I am **saved** and receive God's **favor** through **Christ** and _____

A good work ethic	A regular study time	Extra niceness
A regular prayer time	Tithing	Attending church
Volunteering	Perfectionism	Avoiding conflict
Being a great parent	Excelling at work	Having lots of friends

I revealed myself to those who did not ask for me; I was found by those who did not seek me. To a nation that did not call on my name, I said,

"Here am I, here am I."

(Isaiah 65:1)

While many of the activities listed above are good and desirable, none provide the basis for receiving salvation or favor. It's tempting to look at the Jewish people and think, *How could they miss it?* But sometimes we miss it, too.

5. Read Romans 10:14–17. What role does Paul say you have in sharing the astounding news of Jesus? What prevents you from sharing about Jesus more often? How can you overcome these hindrances?

Paul explores the possibilities of what could lead the Israelites to reject the good news. Maybe they didn't hear the gospel? Maybe they didn't understand it? Paul explains that God has been continually reaching and pursuing his people, but they have rejected him.

6. Read Romans 10:18–21. Then look up Isaiah 52:7 and Isaiah 53:1. How does the joy of the first passage in Isaiah compare with the frustration of the second passage? When have you shared the good news and experienced such joy? When have you shared the good news and experienced such frustration?

7. What does Romans 10:21 reveal about the character of God? What does it reveal about God's heart toward those who don't know Christ? What does it reveal about God's heart toward you?

DAY 3
Romans 11

Modern translations add chapter breaks throughout each book of the Bible. But it's important to remember that Scripture was originally penned on scrolls without any numerical breaks inserted.

1. Reread Romans 10:21 and Romans 11:1. How are these two passages connected? How does Paul build his argument of God's patience and love toward the Jewish people?

After expressing heartache toward fellow Jews not receiving the good news, Paul turns to the story of Elijah as a source of comfort and encouragement.

2. Read Romans 11:2–10. Why does Paul go out of his way to make sure readers know that the Jewish people are not rejected?

The prophet Elijah reached rock bottom in distress and depression. In that place, he felt isolated, alone, like he was the only one. After a powerful encounter with God on a mountainside, Elijah brings his concerns to God for a second time and God answers him.

3. Read 1 Kings 19:14–18. Why is Elijah so beaten down and discouraged? How does God answer Elijah? When are you tempted to believe you're the only one? Of what truth does God remind Elijah, Paul, and us through this passage about his faithfulness and his mighty work?

At the Festival of First Fruits, also known as the Festival of Weeks or Pentecost, the Jews offered God dough made from grain harvest. Through this offering, the whole harvest became holy — as it all belonged to God.

After recognizing the remnant of those who receive the good news, Paul discusses Israel as a whole. Though Israel had stumbled and resisted God's redemptive plan, even this is interwoven in God's purposes. Their hesitancy has made way for Gentiles or non-Jews to rush toward salvation in Christ. The purpose of the Gentiles racing toward God is to make his goodness and love famous and stir a little healthy envy into God's people, so that they soften their hearts and return to God.

4. **Read Romans 11:11–24. What attitudes does Paul warn against having? How did the Jewish people display these attitudes regarding the invitation of Christ for salvation? Where do you struggle with walking in humility?**

Over the last few chapters of Romans, Paul has been building a discussion and developing an argument that's extraordinary. Namely, the same mercy God extended to the Gentiles when they were disobedient will one day be experienced by the Israelites who are disobedient now.

5. **Read Romans 11:25–32. How does God bring goodness out of heartache in this passage? How does God's response show that he has the final word over sin and death?**

In response, Paul makes an offering of passionate praise to God.

6. Read Romans 11:33–36 and Isaiah 55:7–9. How does Romans 11 show that God's ways are higher than our ways?

7. What astounds you most about God's redemptive plan in this chapter? What's one impossible situation you're facing now? How does Romans 11 challenge you to trust that nothing is beyond God's redemption and miracle-working power?

As you reflect on your personal study
of Romans 9–11, what are the beautiful words
the Holy Spirit has been highlighting to you
through this time? Write or draw them
in the space below.

SESSION

7

WITH
LOVE
COMES
RESPONSIBILITY

ROMANS

Opening Group Activity [10-15 MINUTES]

What you'll need:

▶ Sheet of blank paper for each person

▶ Pens

1. Create two columns on the paper. In the first column, list what you most wish Christians were known for today. In the second column, list what you most wish Christians were not known for today.

2. Discuss the following questions:

   ● What do you want Christians to be known for?

   ● What are Christians too often known for today?

   ● Read Romans 12:9–21. How would obeying this instruction as individuals and collectively as the church change the way the world views and engages Christians? Which of these instructions do you need to follow the most right now?

Session Seven Video [20:00 MINUTES]

NOTES: *As you watch, take notes on anything that stands out to you.*

▶ **The will of God isn't something you cherry-pick at a buffet. The will of God becomes clear when you live a life of worship.**

▶ **Don't be conformed to the world. Be renewed. Then you'll know the will of God. This is how we get clarity in crisis.**

> Our gifts function best when we are most yielded to God.

> If you look at how the Trinity functions, you see submission. You have Jesus Christ, the Son who is fully God, but submitted to the Father. And the Holy Spirit, who's fully God, but submitted to the Son. Paul says submission is just a part of how believers function, because submission has to do with order.

> We don't get to be demeaning and belittling to people we disagree with because our God has called us to a higher standard.

> Can you imagine how the world is impacted when we're trying to invite them to a soul-saving, life-changing gospel, but we can't even agree on which day to have church, the style of music, or if you have holes in the jeans you wear to church?

> If Jesus Christ could bear your reproach, surely you can bear the weakness of another brother or a sister in Christ.

Group Discussion Questions [30-45 MINUTES]

1. Read Romans 12:1. What does it look like for you to place your whole life, everything you crave and desire, including your whole heart, mind, soul, and strength, before God as a living offering? What is holding you back from fully presenting your whole self to God right now? What are the benefits of giving your whole self to God? How does this provide clarity in crisis?

2. Read Romans 12:2. In what area of your life do you most long to know God's will for your life? What does this passage reveal about knowing and walking in the fullness of God's will?

3. Jada explains Romans 13:1–5,

> "God is saying, 'I need you to trust me more than you distrust them. Even though authorities are fallen, broken, and they have their own agenda, do you trust me more? Are you rejecting the way of the world, being renewed in your mind, presenting yourself a living sacrifice, knowing my will, using your gifts, and staying humble?'"

How would you answer these questions? Where do you struggle to submit most with governing authorities? On a scale of 1 to 10, how hard is it for you to trust God more than you distrust them? Do you believe that even when authorities fail, God can still accomplish his will? Why or why not? How does a believer's response to authority affect their witness of Jesus?

4. Read Romans 14:1–4. When have you been tempted to mistake a good discipline for doctrine? When have you taught a religious preference to someone else as principle? When have you used your liberty to cause another to stumble? Describe a time when you've given up doing something to love another believer well? What was the result?

5. Read Romans 14:13–19. List some of the hot topics leading toward division in Christianity today.

   How can you respond to a controversial topic in a manner and tone that encourages other believers rather than tears them down? How can you extend grace and compassion to others regarding the non-essentials of faith?

6. Read Romans 15:5–7. How can you become an ambassador of harmony and unity among believers? How does living in harmony and unity with believers who are different from you help declare the gospel?

Close in Prayer

Consider the following prompts as you pray together for:

▸ Awareness of any areas we're holding back from God

▸ Discernment so freedom in Christ doesn't cause stumbling

▸ Unity and harmony among believers.

This *presenting* of our whole lives to God is not a one-time thing; it's an *ongoing* way we show our *love, worship,* and *acceptable service* to God.

Preparation

To prepare for the next group session:

1. Read Romans 12:1–15:12.

2. Tackle the three days of the Session 7 Personal Study.

3. Memorize this week's passage using the Beautiful Word Scripture memory coloring page. As a bonus, look up the Scripture memory passage in different translations and take note of the variations.

4. If you've agreed to bring something for the next session's Opening Group Activity, get it ready.

Therefore, I urge you, brothers and sisters, in view of God's mercy, to offer your bodies as a living sacrifice, holy and pleasing to God — this is your true and proper worship.

—Romans 12:1

PERSONAL
STUDY TIME

DIGGING INTO THE

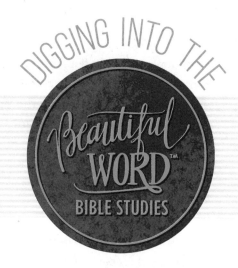

ROMANS
WITH LOVE COMES RESPONSIBILITY

In Greek, the term **bodies** was often seen in terms of **temple sacrifices.** The Hebrew understanding of **body** alluded to the **entire person.**

DAY 1
Romans 12

Considering God's abundant grace, astounding mercy, and gift of salvation, Paul now calls us to practice righteousness. The sacrifice of Jesus and our response to the generous invitation of God places us in right relationship with God. Filled with the Holy Spirit, we are empowered to live in ways that are pleasing to God.

1. Read Romans 12:1–2. What does it mean for you to be a living sacrifice? What does it look like for you to be holy and pleasing to God? What changes do you need to make to reflect these more?

2. What do you most resist surrendering to God? Why? Reflecting on the previous chapters in Romans, what would happen if you surrendered this to God? How does surrendering lead to clarity in life?

3. Read Romans 12:3–8. What spiritual gifts have others mentioned they see in you? How are you using those gifts? Whose spiritual gifts do you find yourself wishing you had? How can you celebrate people who have them instead?

4. What's a way you serve others that brings you the most joy? Do you see this as a spiritual gift? Why or why not? What prevents you from practicing this type of service more frequently?

Never mistake the simplicity of Paul's instruction regarding living in righteousness for its power.

5. Read Romans 12:9–21. Of Paul's vibrant list of ways to love in action, what are the top five that are most meaningful to you today?

-
-
-
-
-

Of Paul's vibrant list of ways to love in action, which are the hardest for you right now? What makes them so difficult?

-
-
-
-
-

6. If you followed everything Paul advises in this passage, how would your life be different? How would your relationships be different?

7. In the space below, write a prayer asking God that through the power of the Holy Spirit and Christ's work on the cross you can live righteously every day.

DAY 2
Romans 13

The Roman Empire was an authoritative government that ruled by power and military might. Anyone viewed as stirring up trouble against the empire was brutally shut down. Citizens were expected to engage in emperor cult worship. The Jews and Christians (who were viewed by the government as a sect of the Jews), were exempt, allowing them to only worship God.

Paul knew the threat and penalties of government authorities firsthand. He had been beaten multiple times by the Romans (Acts 16:16–24; 2 Corinthians 11:24) and acknowledged that there would be times when it's appropriate to obey God rather than human authorities (Acts 5:29). But he also knew the importance of obeying human authority to preserve one's reputation as a child of God. If he was a wild lawbreaker, his influence and witness would diminish. But as an innocent martyr, his influence and witness of Christ would live long beyond him.

1. Read Romans 13:1–7. Why is Paul so concerned about believers' response to their government? How does a believer's response to a government reveal or undermine their witness to Christ?

2. Do you tend to view your citizenship in terms of the country where you live or God's kingdom? How does that perspective shape how you respond and speak of your local, state, or federal government?

3. Read Romans 13:8–10. Paul writes that our ongoing debt is to love one another, and that true love never hurts someone else. What's your go-to response for unlovable people? What can you do to grow a more loving, patient, gracious response toward them?

4. Who is someone you'd like to get back at or snap back at right now? What does this passage challenge you to do instead?

5. Who is someone you know you've hurt in the past month, by what you've done or said or left undone or unsaid? How can you make the relationship right?

The first half of the Ten Commandments centers on loving God and the second half centers on loving others.

6. Read Romans 13:11–14. Where are you slumbering in your spiritual journey? What do you need to do to wake up?

7. What do the following Scriptures reveal about clothing yourself in Christlikeness? How can you clothe yourself in Christ today?

Galatians 3:26–27:

Ephesians 4:22–24:

Colossians 3:12–14:

DAY 3
Romans 14:1-15:12

1. Read Romans 14:1–4. How do you respond to believers who have a more black-and-white, rules-based approach to faith than you? How do you respond to believers who have a grayer, more grace-based approach to faith than you? What does this passage say your response should be?

2. Read Romans 14:5–6. What do those two sets of believers have wildly different views on?

3. On the continuum below, mark how you tend to respond to followers of Jesus whose views on faith and life differ a lot from yours. How are you demonstrating love, compassion, and acceptance of these believers? How can you make space for more of these believers in your everyday life?

◀ 1 2 3 4 5 6 7 8 9 10 ▶

I tend to withdraw from or judge believers whose perspectives are wildly different from mine.

I draw close to believers whose perspectives are wildly different from mine.

4. Read Romans 14:7–12. How can you resist compromising your faith and yet still show great kindness and compassion? In what area of life do you find yourself struggling with this most?

Therefore judge nothing before the appointed time; wait until the Lord comes. He will bring to light what is hidden in darkness and will expose the motives of the heart. At that time each will receive their praise from God.

I Corinthians 4:5

5. Place a star by the phrases below that best describe you now. Circle the phrases you want fellow believers to use to describe you.

I want to be right.	I want to be righteous.
I want to win the argument	The argument isn't as important as loving well.
I need to correct the person.	I trust the Spirit to guide and lead the person in truth.
My doctrine is perfect.	I have a lot to learn as I grow closer to Jesus.
My desire is most important.	My desire is to bring out the best in others.
I don't care if they don't like it.	I want to make sure no one stumbles because of me.

In the Roman Empire, where emperor worship was required, many of the butcher shops were part of pagan temples. A portion of the meat was sacrificed through burning, and the rest was sold to the public. Jewish communities had their own butchers to ensure none of the meat had been sacrificed to false gods. Some Jewish Christians became vegetarians to ensure they didn't accidentally eat meat that had been sacrificed to idols.

6. Read Romans 14:13–23. When beliefs collide, what does Paul call you to do? (vv. 13, 15–16, 19, 22) Which of these is easiest for you? Which of these is hardest for you? Why?

7. Read Romans 15:1–12. What is one relationship you have had that soured because of differing beliefs? What steps can you take to bring healing and harmony to this relationship?

As you reflect on your personal study of Romans 12:1–15:12, what are the beautiful words the Holy Spirit has been highlighting to you through this time? Write or draw them in the space below.

A HOPE
THAT HELPS YOU
ENDURE

ROMANS

Opening Group Activity [10-15 MINUTES]

▶ Each person to bring food to share

▶ Party balloons or fun decorations

1. Decorate the room with balloons, streamers, wildflowers, and anything you can find to create a festive atmosphere.

2. Enjoy laughing, talking, sharing, and catching up as you eat together.

3. Discuss the following:

   ● What have you enjoyed most about the book of Romans?

   ● What's one question or topic from the homework or discussion that really challenged you or stuck with you?

Session Two Video [18:00 MINUTES]

NOTES: *As you watch, take notes on anything that stands out to you.*

⟫ **Hope isn't found in a career, education, heritage, or good circumstances; it's only in God.**

⟫ **When we minister to others, we need to commend people, reminding them that we see their good work and the evidence of what God is doing through them.**

What made you reflect? What

surprised you?

What caught your attention? What

❯ God is working in and through you in word and deed, not just the things you say but the way you live your life.

❯ God might not be holding something back because you're in sin or because something's wrong, but because he has a greater call on your life.

❯ Phoebe is a reminder to all singles that there's a call on your life, even greater than marriage.

❯ Sanctification, holiness, and righteousness are important, and yet there's a power beyond us in the Holy Spirit that allows us to abound in hope.

Group Discussion Questions [30-45 MINUTES]

1. Read Romans 15:13–14. Throughout his letter, Paul has delivered some challenging truths, but now he commends the Roman believers. How often do you commend others by calling out their gifts, good works, and the ways you see God working in their lives? When was the last time someone commended you for your faith and good works? Who are three people you can reach out to this week to encourage and commend?

2. Reflecting on Romans 15:22–24, Jada teaches,

> "Maybe you want to be **married**, or maybe you want to have **kids**, or maybe you **envision** some certain life for **yourself.** Those things are not bad things, but God may put those longings on **hold** because there's a **greater** call on your life."

Describe a time when God worked on a different timetable than you chose, but now you recognize God was doing something good. How does this encourage you to trust God in your current longings that remain unfulfilled?

3. Read Romans 16:1–2. Phoebe is single and yet is used by God as a deaconess and financial backer of the church. Sometimes the surrounding culture tempts us to believe that because our lives don't follow the common life script—marriage, kids, profession—that somehow, we're less significant. What's one area where your life hasn't followed the common script? How have you grown in faith in this area? How has God used you to impact others through this?

4. Jada teaches,

"When we see political headlines, the things happening with social justice, the tensions in our family, the things we wrestle with in our heart, the job we may be wanting, or the medical issues or financial issues we struggle with, I want you to ask, 'How does Romans change the way I look at it?'"

Where have you been struggling and then found clarity in the teachings of Romans?

_____

_____

_____

_____

_____

_____

_____

_____

_____

_____

_____

_____

_____

_____

5. Reflecting on the discussion and notes from the previous sessions, how has your faith grown through Romans? What are you most excited to share about God with others because of this study? What changes do you need to make to live with more clarity every day?

6. How would you sum up the book of Romans in a few words? What's the most beautiful aspect of Romans to you? What's your biggest takeaway from this Beautiful Word study? How will you live your life differently because of this discovery?

Close in Prayer

Consider the following prompts as you pray together for:

▶ Increased clarity in every area of life

▶ Renewed hope in areas of disappointment

▶ Thriving spiritual friendships and relationships

Hope is found in God alone.

Preparation

To conclude this study:

1. Read Romans 15:13–16.

2. Tackle the three days of the Session 8 Personal Study.

3. Memorize this week's passage using the Beautiful Word Scripture memory coloring page. As a bonus, look up the Scripture memory passage in different translations and take note of the variations.

May the God of hope fill you with all joy and peace as you trust in him, so that you may overflow with hope by the power of the Holy Spirit.

—Romans 15:13

SESSION

8

PERSONAL

STUDY TIME

DIGGING INTO THE

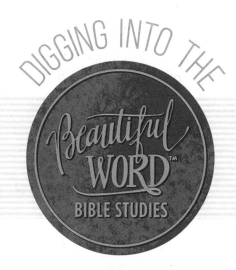

Beautiful WORD™ BIBLE STUDIES

ROMANS

A HOPE THAT HELPS YOU ENDURE

DAY 1
Romans 15:13–31

Midway through Romans 15, Paul commends his readers and shares his desire for time together.

1. Read Romans 15:13–22. How does Paul balance out corrective words in Romans with this commendation?

2. How does Paul show his affection in this passage?

One of the proofs that Christ has been working in Paul is the power of signs and wonders through the Holy Spirit. In the Old Testament, signs and wonders were used to reveal God's presence and power. Israel witnessed many miracles throughout their history, including the Exodus and wilderness experiences. Jesus performed countless miracles (John 21:25) and God continues to demonstrate his presence through signs and wonders today.

3. Read Romans 15:19 and Acts 11:12. How did the signs and wonders that followed Paul help him spread the gospel? What does 1 Corinthians 12:8–10 reveal about God using signs and wonders today?

The "goodness" Paul acknowledges in

Romans 15:15

is a facet of the

fruit

of the

Spirit

(Galatians 5:22).

4. Read Romans 15:23–29. How important are relationships to Paul in this passage? How much of a priority do you place on spending time with fellow believers outside of a church service? Who comes to mind?

5. Read Romans 15:30–31. On the continuum below, mark how hard it is to share personal prayer requests about yourself? Do you tend to ask people to pray for someone you know or your own needs? Why?

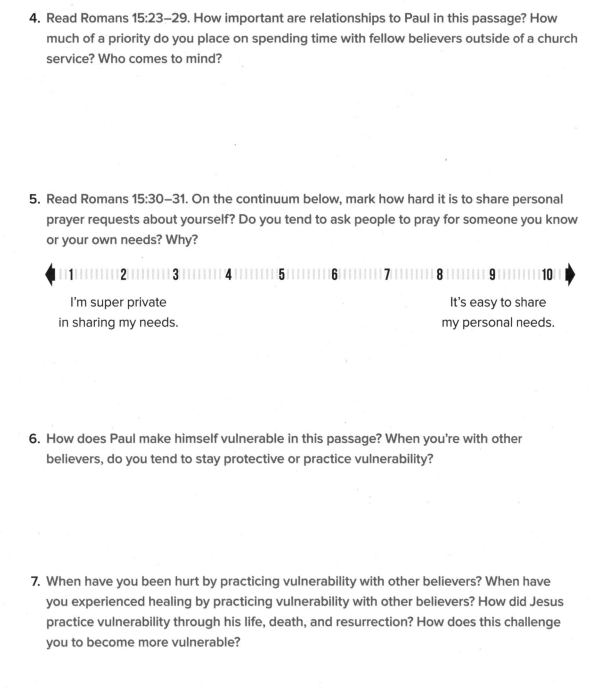

| 1   2   3   4   5   6   7   8   9   10 |

I'm super private
in sharing my needs.

It's easy to share
my personal needs.

6. How does Paul make himself vulnerable in this passage? When you're with other believers, do you tend to stay protective or practice vulnerability?

7. When have you been hurt by practicing vulnerability with other believers? When have you experienced healing by practicing vulnerability with other believers? How did Jesus practice vulnerability through his life, death, and resurrection? How does this challenge you to become more vulnerable?

DAY 2
Romans 16

The closing chapter provides a beautiful bookend to Romans. Paul begins by giving shoutouts and instructions to specific leaders and supporters before once again calling believers to unity.

1. Read Romans 16:1–2. What does Paul's gratitude toward Phoebe at the top of this list reveal about Paul's attitude about women serving in the church?

Phoebe means "BRIGHT" or "RADIANT"

2. When have you second-guessed your significance and value because of your gender, finances, or marital status? How does Paul's commendation encourage you?

3. Romans 16:3–15. Reflecting on the kind words Paul writes to each person, what are the top three statements you'd like people to say of you?

-
-
-

4. How can you live in such a way that makes others experience these traits in you?

5. Read Romans 16:16–23. What does Paul accomplish by sending greetings from other people? What's one practical way you can nurture unity and connection among believers?

Some of Priscilla and Aquila's travels with Paul are described in **Acts 18:2, 24-28.**

6. Read Romans 16:24–27. How does this closing sum up what Paul has been teaching throughout Romans?

7. Paul could have chosen any characteristics of God for his closing. He selects *only* and *wise*. In what way has Romans revealed God as the only God and a wise God to you?

DAY 3
Your Beautiful Word

Review your notes and responses throughout this study guide. Place a star by those that stand out to you. Then respond to the following questions:

1. What's one thing you never knew about Romans that you know now? How has that knowledge impacted you?

2. What are three of the most important truths you learned from studying Romans?

3. After reviewing the eight Beautiful Word coloring pages, which one stands out to you the most? Why?

4. What's one practical application from the study that you've put into practice? What's one practical application from the study that you still need to do?

5. What changes have you noticed in your attitudes, actions, and behaviors because of studying Romans?

6. How are you treating or responding to others differently because of this study?

7. How are you living with greater clarity because of this study?

As you reflect on your personal study of Romans 15:14–16:27, what are the beautiful words the Holy Spirit has been highlighting to you through this time? Write or draw them in the space below.

_____

_____

_____

_____

_____

_____

_____

_____

_____

_____

_____

_____

_____

_____

_____

_____

_____

_____

_____

_____

_____

SCRIPTURE MEMORY CARDS

SESSION 1

"THROUGH HIM WE RECEIVED GRACE AND APOSTLESHIP TO CALL ALL THE GENTILES TO THE OBEDIENCE THAT COMES FROM FAITH FOR HIS NAME'S SAKE."

—Romans 1:5

SESSION 2

"FOR I AM NOT ASHAMED OF THE GOSPEL, BECAUSE IT IS THE POWER OF GOD THAT BRINGS SALVATION TO EVERYONE WHO BELIEVES: FIRST TO THE JEW, THEN TO THE GENTILE."

—Romans 1:16

SESSION 3

"THIS RIGHTEOUSNESS IS GIVEN THROUGH FAITH IN JESUS CHRIST TO ALL WHO BELIEVE. THERE IS NO DIFFERENCE BETWEEN JEW AND GENTILE, FOR ALL HAVE SINNED AND FALL SHORT OF THE GLORY OF GOD,"

—Romans 3:22–23

SESSION 4

"NOW IF WE DIED WITH CHRIST, WE BELIEVE THAT WE WILL ALSO LIVE WITH HIM."

—Romans 6:8

SCRIPTURE MEMORY CARDS

SESSION 5

"FOR THOSE WHO ARE LED BY THE SPIRIT OF GOD ARE THE CHILDREN OF GOD."

—Romans 8:14

SESSION 6

"FOR HE SAYS TO MOSES, 'I WILL HAVE MERCY ON WHOM I HAVE MERCY, AND I WILL HAVE COMPASSION ON WHOM I HAVE COMPASSION.'"

—Romans 9:15

SESSION 7

"THEREFORE, I URGE YOU, BROTHERS AND SISTERS, IN VIEW OF GOD'S MERCY, TO OFFER YOUR BODIES AS A LIVING SACRIFICE, HOLY AND PLEASING TO GOD—THIS IS YOUR TRUE AND PROPER WORSHIP."

—Romans 12:1

SESSION 8

"MAY THE GOD OF HOPE FILL YOU WITH ALL JOY AND PEACE AS YOU TRUST IN HIM, SO THAT YOU MAY OVERFLOW WITH HOPE BY THE POWER OF THE HOLY SPIRIT."

—Romans 15:13

ABOUT THE AUTHOR

Jada Edwards is an experienced Bible teacher, author, and speaker who has committed her life to equipping women of all ages with practical, biblical truth. Alongside her husband, Conway Edwards, the Senior Pastor, she serves as the Women's Pastor and Director of Creative Services at One Community Church in Plano, Texas. Jada teaches women's Bible study, is the author of multiple books, a contributing teacher In the Known by Name Bible study series, and author of *Galatians: Accepted and Free*. She and her husband have a son, Joah, and a daughter, Chloe.

ENDNOTE

1 Lucado, Max. *Life Lessons from Romans* (Nashville: Thomas Nelson, 2018), 66

Discover the Beauty of God's Word

The Beautiful Word™ Bible Study Series helps you connect God's Word to your daily life through vibrant video teaching, group discussion, and deep personal study that includes verse-by-verse reading, Scripture memory, coloring pages, and encouragement to receive your own beautiful Word from God.

In each study, a central theme—a beautiful word—threads throughout the book, helps you connect and apply each book of the Bible to your daily life today, and forever.

IN THIS SERIES:

GALATIANS — Jada Edwards — Available Now
REVELATION — Margaret Feinberg — Available Now
EPHESIANS — Lori Wilhite — Available Now
ROMANS — Jada Edwards — Available Now
PHILIPPIANS — Lori Wilhite — Fall 2022
JOHN — Megan Fate Marshman — Winter 2022
LUKE — Lisa Harper — Spring 2023

Study Guide
9780310115410

Study Guide
9780310122388

Study Guide
with Streaming Video
9780310130949

These Bible studies, along with Beautiful Word™ Bibles and Bible Journals are available wherever books are sold. Streaming video available on StudyGateway.com.

Harper Christian Resources